ARTIFACT CASE STUDIES

Interpreting Children's Work and Teachers' Classroom Strategies

Jeanne Ellis Ormrod

University of Northern Colorado (Emerita)

University of New Hampshire

PEARSON

Merrill
Prentice Hall

Upper Saddle River, New Jersey
Columbus, Ohio

KH

Vice President and Executive Publisher: Jeffery W. Johnston
Publisher: Kevin M. Davis
Editorial Assistant: Amanda King
Production Editor: Mary Harlan
Cover Design: Ali Mohrman
Production Manager: Laura Messerly
Director of Marketing: Ann Castel Davis
Marketing Manager: Autumn Purdy
Marketing Coordinator: Tyra Poole

Pearson Prentice Hall™ is a trademark of Pearson Education, Inc.
Pearson® is a registered trademark of Pearson plc
Prentice Hall® is a registered trademark of Pearson Education, Inc.
Merrill® is a registered trademark of Pearson Education, Inc.

Pearson Education Ltd.
Pearson Education Singapore Pte. Ltd.
Pearson Education Canada, Ltd.
Pearson Education--Japan

Pearson Education Australia Pty. Limited
Pearson Education North Asia Ltd.
Pearson Educación de Mexico, S.A. de C.V.
Pearson Education Malaysia Pte. Ltd.

8 9 10 11 12 V036 12
ISBN: 0-13-114671-8

3/26/14

Preface

I have written this book to serve as a companion to textbooks in educational psychology, child development, and similar disciplines. More specifically, I've written it to help students in teacher education and other professional programs apply psychological concepts and principles related to learning, motivation, development, instruction, and assessment. To assist instructors who are using the book for the first time, I've written an accompanying *Instructor's Manual* that can be obtained by calling Faculty Support at 1-800-526-0485 or by requesting a copy from your local Prentice Hall representative.

All of the artifacts included here have come from preschool, elementary school, middle school, and high school classrooms, and I am most appreciative of the students, educators, and parents who have graciously allowed me to use their work. In particular, I wish to thank the Belcher family, Don Burger, Chris Cairns, the Davis family, Barbara Dee, the Gass family, Darrell Harris, Rita Hocog Inos, Don Lafferty, Teresa McDevitt, Meghan Milligan, Jay Pawlyk, Julie Peters, Ann Reilly, the Rourke family, the Sheehan family, Ann Shump, Helen Snelson, Drew Spencer, Jennifer Taylor, Grace Tober, Sally Tossey, Kris Wright, and Geoff Wuehrmann.

I am always eager for feedback from instructors and students; it is only by getting such feedback that I can continue to improve my work. Please feel free to send your comments to me at jormrod@alumni.brown.edu.

J.E.O.

Contents

Introduction to the Artifact Cases 1

Table of Grade Levels, Content Areas, and Relevant Theoretical Domains 2

Preschool

Artifact 1   Penguins 3

Artifact 2   Google Glasses 5

Early Elementary Grades (K–2)

Artifact 3   Numbers 7

Artifact 4   Book Report 10

Artifact 5   Interview with Maggie 12

Artifact 6   Homework 15

Artifact 7   Wonders of Weather 17

Artifact 8   Magical Sea Monsters 20

Upper Elementary Grades (3–5)

Artifact 9   Perspectives 22

Artifact 10   Self-Reflection #1 24

Artifact 11   Snow 26

Artifact 12   Watercolor Rubric 30

Artifact 13   Spelling Test 32

Artifact 14   New Year's Resolutions 34

Artifact 15   A Really Bad Day 37

Middle School Grades (6–8)

Artifact 16   Self-Reflection #2 40

Artifact 17   Trees 42

Artifact 18   Friends 46

Artifact 19   Clifford's Tower 49

Artifact 20   Taking Notes 52

Artifact 21   Math Quiz 55

Artifact 22   Variables 57

Artifact 23   Holocaust Museum 59

High School Grades (9–12)

Artifact 24   The Three A's 62

Artifact 25   Dark Magic 64

Artifact 26   The Boy Code 69

Artifact 27   Shadowing 72

Artifact 28   The War of 1812 76

Artifact 29   Dropping Out 79

Artifact 30   Common Standards 82

Introduction to the Artifact Cases

As someone who is preparing to be a teacher or other professional who works with young people, you have probably encountered case studies in your textbooks and other contexts. Typically, such case studies take the form of stories about particular events in schools and classrooms. This book offers case studies of a different sort. In particular, it presents *artifact cases*—work samples and instructional materials that, in their own way, tell "stories" about children, adolescents, and teachers.

The book contains thirty artifact cases. Each one includes one or more items that a student or teacher has created—perhaps a drawing, essay, test, questionnaire, brochure, or evaluation instrument—and each one can potentially tell us something about its creator. In every case, I give you some background information and ask you several questions to consider as you examine the artifact(s) presented. My questions are designed to help you apply concepts and principles you have learned in a class in educational psychology, child development, or similar discipline. As you will soon discover, concepts and principles related to learning, thinking, motivation, cognitive and social development, instruction, and assessment will often help you better understand what a child or teacher has done.

The artifact cases in this book cover a broad age range, from preschool to high school. Some are specific to particular content areas—literacy, mathematics, science, social studies, or art—while others are more general in nature. The table on the following page indicates the grade level, content areas, and theoretical domains (learning, motivation, social development, etc.) to which each artifact is relevant.

Table of Grade Levels, Content Areas, and Relevant Theoretical Domains

Artifact	Preschool	K-2	3-5	6-8	9-12	General	Literacy	Math	Science	Social Studies	Art	Learning & Cognition	Motivation	Cognitive Development	Language Development	Personal/Social Development	Special Needs	Objectives & Standards	Instructional Strategies	Classroom Management	Assessment
#1: Penguins	√							√				√							√		√
#2: Google Glasses	√										√	√	√	√					√		
#3: Numbers		√						√				√		√							√
#4: Book Report		√					√							√		√					
#5: Interview with Maggie		√				√						√		√							√
#6: Homework		√				√								√						√	
#7: Wonders of Weather		√						√	√			√							√	√	√
#8: Magical Sea Monsters		√					√					√				√					
#9: Perspectives			√			√								√		√			√		
#10: Self-Reflection #1			√			√						√	√	√		√	√				
#11: Snow			√				√					√							√		
#12: Watercolor Rubric			√								√										√
#13: Spelling Test			√				√							√				√			√
#14: New Year's Resolutions			√			√							√			√					
#15: Really Bad Day			√				√											√	√	√	√
#16: Self-Reflection #2				√		√						√	√	√		√					√
#17: Trees				√					√			√							√		
#18: Friends				√		√										√					
#19: Clifford's Tower				√						√		√							√	√	
#20: Taking Notes				√		√	√					√		√					√		
#21: Math Quiz				√				√				√						√	√		√
#22: Variables				√			√		√			√		√							
#23: Holocaust Museum				√						√		√	√						√		
#24: Three A's					√	√	√					√	√								√
#25: Dark Magic					√		√							√							√
#26: Boy Code					√	√	√			√		√				√		√			
#27: Shadowing					√	√						√	√			√					
#28: War of 1812					√					√		√		√					√		
#29: Dropping Out					√		√					√	√		√	√				√	√
#30: Common Standards					√	√						√		√	√	√			√		√

Artifact #1

Penguins

In her preschool class, 3½-year-old Katie completes a worksheet on which she matches the numbers of dots on penguins to various numerals. The worksheet is shown on the following page.

Questions to Consider as You Examine the Worksheet

- What cognitive process(es) does the task involve?

- What are the benefits of such a worksheet?

- What are the weaknesses of the worksheet?

- Without knowing anything about the context in which the worksheet is being used, would you characterize it as (a) an instructional aid or (b) an assessment instrument?

Artifact #2

Google Glasses

Working at home, 4½-year-old Drew imagines, and then draws, night-vision glasses that he calls "google glasses." After drawing the glasses, he tells his mother all about his invention, and she writes his explanations on the drawing. Drew's google glasses appear on the next page.

Questions to Consider as You Examine the Drawing

- Judging from other preschoolers' drawings you may have seen in the past, would you say that Drew's artwork is typical or atypical for his age-group?

- If you had to predict that Drew might eventually require special educational services to help him reach his full potential, in which category of special needs might you place him?

- Look at the specific features that Drew includes in his glasses. What hypotheses might you form about Drew's interests and prior experiences?

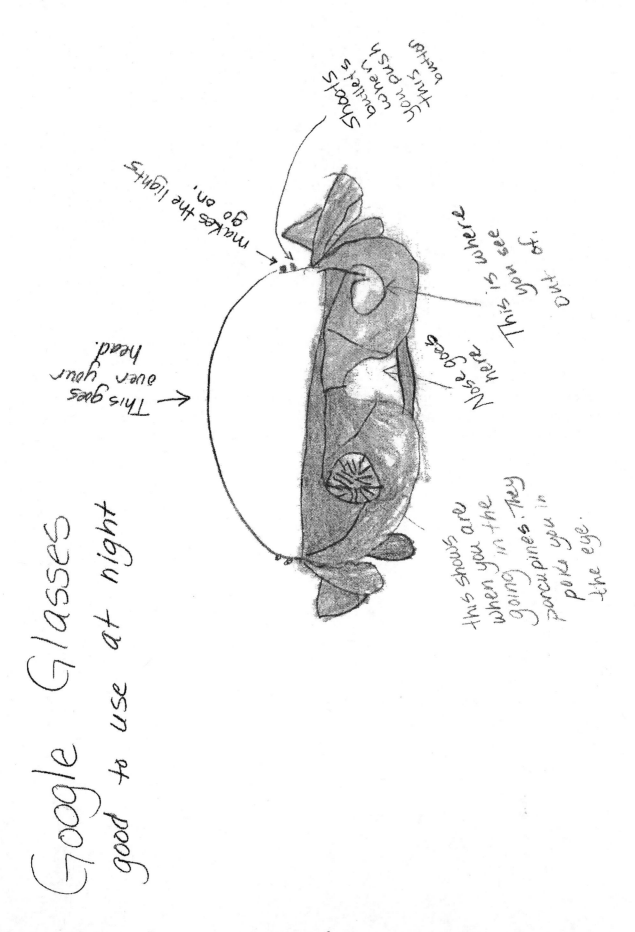

Google Glasses
good to use at night

This goes over your head.

Makes the lights go on.

Shoots out when you push Shoots

This is where you see out of.

Nose goes here

This shoots are when you are going in the porcupines. They poke you in the eye.

Artifact #3

Numbers

Twice during the school year—once in October and once in February—a kindergarten teacher asks 5-year-old Meghan to write the numbers 1 through 20. The teacher then asks Meghan to begin at 1 and count as high as she can. Meghan's performance on both occasions is included in her portfolio at the end of the school year. The relevant pages from the portfolio, reproduced at their original sizes, are shown on the following two pages.

Questions to Consider as You Examine the Portfolio Entries

- What things does Meghan appear to have learned about the number system? What things has she not yet learned?

- What differences do you see between Meghan's performances during the two assessments? What might these differences indicate?

- What benefits might showing Meghan's performance over time have for Meghan? for her parents? for her teacher?

Performance in October

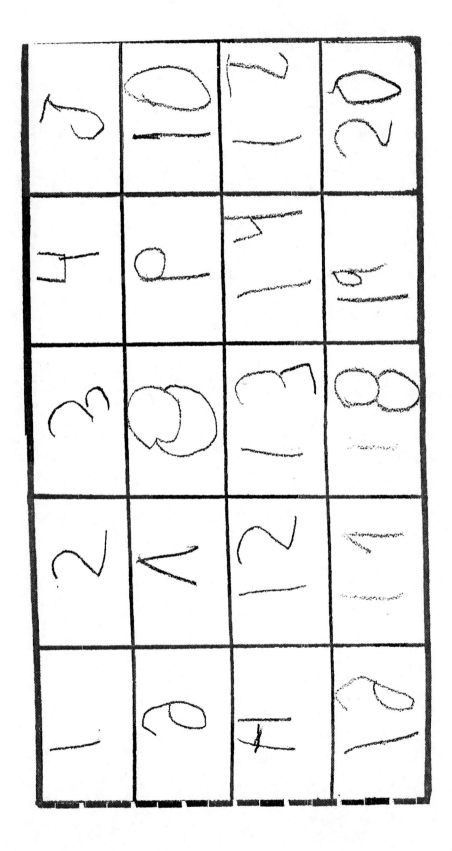

1	2	3	4
6	7	8	9	10
14	12	13	14	12
12	18	19	20

COUNTS BY ROTE TO 39

8

Performance in February

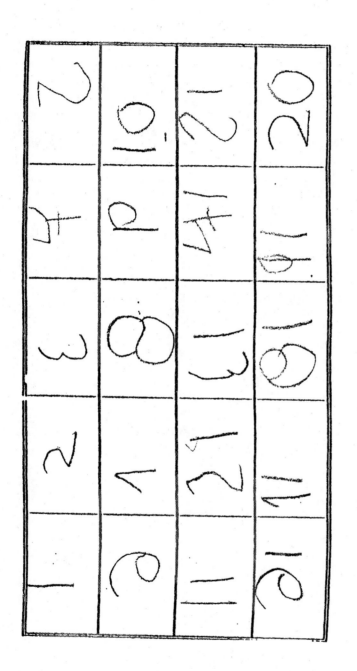

1	2	3	4	2
3	7	8	9	10
11	12	13	14	12
12	19	18	19	20

COUNTS BY ROTE TO <u>99</u>

Said "I don't know what's next".

9

Artifact #4

Book Report

Seven-year-old Andrew has been diagnosed with attention-deficit hyperactivity disorder (ADHD), a condition characterized by distractibility, hyperactive and impulsive behavior, or a combination of these symptoms. Despite his disability, Andrew is a likeable boy with many friends, and he excels at such sports as baseball and soccer.

For an assignment in his first-grade class, Andrew listens to a tape of Jan Brett's *The Wild Christmas Reindeer*.[1] He then completes a "Reading Log" to describe the book. Andrew's reading log is shown on the following page. In small print, his teacher writes what he is trying to say.

Questions to Consider as You Examine the Reading Log

- Do you think that such writing is typical of first graders? Recall instances of 6- and 7-year-olds' writing you've seen in the past to make a reasonable guess.

- What aspects of written language has Andrew mastered?

- What aspects of written language has Andrew *not* mastered?

- Might this writing sample lead you to suspect that Andrew has another disability either instead of or in addition to ADHD? If so, what type of disability might he have?

---

[1] *The Wild Christmas Reindeer,* by J. Brett, 1990, New York: Penguin.

Reading Log

Name: Andre Date: W 21

Title: In a wild ___ or ___

Author: JAN BRETT

☒ listening center ☐ partner
name:
☐ adult
name:
☐ independent

Three important things about the story: RWF

1. I LTHE PWNEPL RWFa

  I like the part when she got the reindeer ready.

2. ELTHEPRTVNPTOCAm

  she took them to the corral.

3. THEPWN SANDICAme. *(asked what does silent mean)*

Connections ▨ This story reminds me of this CHRISTHAS

Artifact #5

Interview with Maggie

To fulfill an assignment for his course in educational psychology, graduate student Kris Wright conducts an interview with 7-year-old Maggie about the nature of learning and thinking. The interview appears on the next two pages.

Questions to Consider as You Read the Interview

- Kris's first few questions yield little information from Maggie (she responds with "I don't know" or "Yeah"). Why might Maggie initially have difficulty describing what she is learning in school?

- What strategies does Kris use to probe Maggie's knowledge and beliefs about learning and thinking?

- What does the interview reveal about Maggie's understanding of learning and thinking?

Kris:	Are you learning a lot in school?
Maggie:	I don't know.
Kris:	It's hard to say?
Maggie:	Yeah.
Kris:	Why?
Maggie:	I don't know.
Kris:	How do you know when you've learned something?
Maggie:	Because in the book it says stuff and then we go on.
Kris:	When you've learned something, what is it that you do that makes you know you've learned it?
Maggie:	I don't know.
Kris:	What kinds of things do you learn in school?
Maggie:	How to write in cursive.
Kris:	How do you know you've learned to write in cursive?
Maggie:	Because it's in our spelling book. It says how to write.
Kris:	When do you know you've learned something?
Maggie:	Because it's in this little notebook.
Kris:	Do you write it in the notebook?
Maggie:	Yeah.
Kris:	What kinds of things do you write in there?
Maggie:	Spelling words.
Kris:	Can you give me some examples?
Maggie:	Well, we've had *chin* and *chair* and *each* and words that have "ch." Then we have a test.
Kris:	Do you do well on your tests?
Maggie:	Yeah.
Kris:	Does that mean that you've learned those words?
Maggie:	Yeah.
Kris:	How does your teacher let you know you're supposed to learn what the teacher is telling you?
Maggie:	She tells us to pay attention.
Kris:	What does it mean to pay attention?
Maggie:	Listening.

Kris:	Can you do other things while you listen?
Maggie:	Sometimes I think about what I'm going to do when I go home. Like what we're going to have for supper.
Kris:	Is it OK for you to talk to a friend while you listen?
Maggie:	No.
Kris:	Why not?
Maggie:	Because that's rude.
Kris:	When you have to remember something like the alphabet, do you do anything special in order to be able to remember all the letters?
Maggie:	Well, we just do them all over and over and over again.
Kris:	Do you do anything else to help you remember them?
Maggie:	Nope.

Kris asks Maggie to recite her ABCs, which she does using the traditional song. Kris then recites them in a monotone.

Kris:	What was different about the way we each said them?
Maggie:	I sang it.
Kris:	Sometimes you put things into a song and it makes it easier to remember?
Maggie:	Yeah.
Kris:	What happens when you try to remember something.
Maggie:	It's just right there.
Kris:	Where does it come from?
Maggie:	My mind.
Kris:	Where is your mind?
Maggie:	In my head.
Kris:	What do you think happens in your mind?
Maggie:	Stuff gets in there and talks to each other and tells me what I want to know.

Artifact #6

Homework

Early in the school year, a second-grade teacher notifies her students' parents that the following week, she will begin to give the children occasional homework assignments. The letter she sends home appears on the following page.

Questions to Consider as You Examine the Letter

- Research to date indicates that doing homework enhances school achievement for older students (e.g., those in the middle school or high school grades) but has little or no effect on the achievement of younger students (especially those in the early elementary school grades). Why, then, do you think the teacher might be giving occasional homework assignments?

- What procedure will the teacher be using for sending home homework assignments? What advantage(s) might this procedure have?

- What critical points does the teacher communicate to parents about doing homework? What other things does she also communicate to them, either explicitly or implicitly?

- How does the teacher suggest that parents contact her about their questions and concerns? What are the advantages of this strategy? the disadvantages?

- How might you modify the note so that it would be appropriate for the parents of middle school students? How might you modify it to be appropriate for the parents of high school students?

Homework

Homework will begin next week. All the work for the week will come home in a green folder on Monday afternoon. Please return the completed work, stapled to the cover sheet, on Friday morning **in the same folder.**

Homework is your child's responsibility. Please help him or her get into a good routine by setting a regular time and providing a quiet place and assistance if necessary. Homework should take only 20 to 30 minutes per night. If it is taking your child more time, please contact me and I will adjust the expectation.

Sometimes, children cannot finish work due to family commitments, sickness, or other legitimate reasons. Please write a note and return it with the cover sheet so that I know what is going on with your child. I'd prefer that unfinished homework not linger on and on and hang over a child's head. There is always another packet the following week and that is usually plenty, so don't fret about some missed work.

I assign what is appropriate for most second graders. However, some children and parents would prefer more homework. Feel free to supplement by reading together every night in addition to the designated reading night and filling out the Reading Record sheet. **However, I never want homework to interfere with family time.** I think that discussions, cuddling, playing a board game, cooking, reading and listening to stories, taking a walk in the woods, and looking at the stars do more to foster cognitive and language development than a worksheet done alone. (Notice that I didn't include television or Nintendo!) I urge you to limit TV time and spend as much time with your child as you can. I figure there will be time to scrub and polish when the children are gone. So much for my lecture! Have fun!

Remember that I try to check my e-mail three times a day. If you have a question or concern, I can get to my computer in the classroom a lot faster than I can leave the room and get to the phone. Here's my impossibly long e-mail address.

[e-mail address appears here]

Artifact #7

Wonders of Weather

In a 3-month unit called "Wonders of Weather" in the science curriculum, a second-grade class in Canada is learning about air and water in the environment. In the unit, the students are studying such topics as wind, temperature, the water cycle, and the need for clean air and water. At three different times during the unit, graduate student Jennifer Taylor meets one-on-one with a second grader named Tom to assess his knowledge and beliefs about air and water. Each time Jennifer meets with Tom, she asks him to construct a *concept map* that shows his current understanding of air, water, and related concepts, as well as how such concepts are interconnected. To create a map, Jennifer and Tom write important concepts (*air*, *water*, *lakes*, *plants*, etc.) on individual Post-It® notes. Tom then arranges the notes on a dry-erase board and indicates relationships among concepts by writing arrows and phrases on the dry-erase board. As his map evolves, Tom occasionally moves a Post-It® note from one place to another and revises the arrows and phrases on the board accordingly. Once Tom has completed a map, Jennifer copies it on a sheet of paper so that she has a permanent record of what he has created.

Tom's three concept maps, constructed at the beginning, middle, and end of the weather unit, are shown on the next two pages.

Questions to Consider as You Examine the Concept Maps

- In what ways does Tom's knowledge about air and water change over the course of the unit?

- What advantages might concept maps have for *promoting* students' learning? What advantages might they have for *assessing* students' learning?

- If you were a teacher using concept maps to assess students' learning, how might you grade (i.e., evaluate and score) such maps? What issues would you need to consider regarding the validity and reliability of the maps?

- School personnel have previously identified Tom as having a special educational need. Based on what you see in the maps, can you guess the special need that school personnel have identified?

Tom's Concept Map at Interview 1

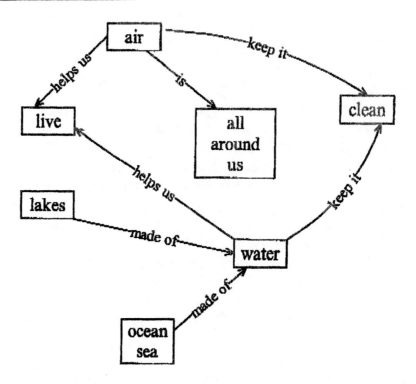

Tom's Concept Map at Interview 2

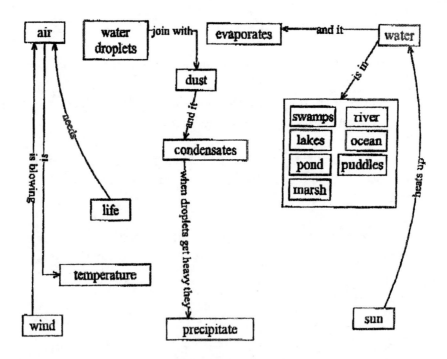

Maps are from *"Because It's My Work": Primary Students' Learning in Elementary Science and Technology*, by J. Taylor, 2001, unpublished master's thesis, Queen's University, Kingston, Ontario, Canada, pp. 91–92; reprinted by permission of the author.

Tom's Concept Map at Interview 3

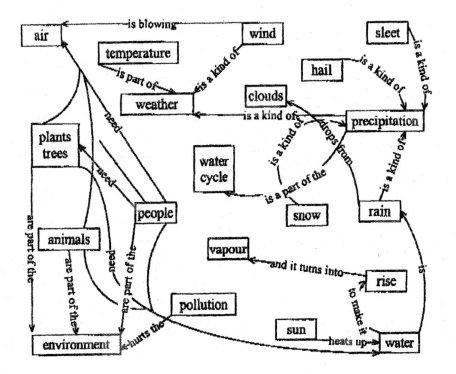

Map is from *"Because It's My Work": Primary Students' Learning in Elementary Science and Technology,* by J. Taylor, 2001, unpublished master's thesis, Queen's University, Kingston, Ontario, Canada, p. 92; reprinted by permission of the author.

Artifact #8

Magical Sea Monsters

A second-grade teacher teaches her students how to make colorful designs on paper using water-soluble markers and water. After their creations have dried, the children cut them into pieces of varying shapes. Next, the children develop stories that their designs and shapes might illustrate.

The children type their stories with word-processing software and use the spell-check feature to edit their spelling. They then "publish" their stories in spiral-bound books. Each book begins with a title page (including the author, name and location of their school, and month and year of publication) and dedication page (e.g., "This book is dedicated to my family and friends"). Following is the story itself (on the left-hand pages) with accompanying illustrations (on the right-hand pages). The children laminate the pages, making their books durable products that will survive many readings.

Eight-year-old Tony's under-the-sea story is inspired by the blue-and-green swirling designs that he has created with the water-soluble markers. His finished product is 16 pages long. His story appears on the next page; the spaces between paragraphs indicate page breaks in his book.

Questions to Consider as You Examine the Story

- What inferences can you draw about Tony's language development and writing skills?

- What aspects of narrative writing has Tony clearly mastered?

- Tony's story is obviously much shorter than one that an experienced novelist might write. In what other ways is it different from that of a professional adult storyteller?

- What cognitive processes are evident in Tony's story?

- If we consider Piaget's theory of cognitive development, we would guess that, as an 8-year-old, Tony is in the concrete operations stage of development. Is Tony's story consistent with Piaget's depiction of concrete operational thinking? Why or why not?

The Magical Sea Monsters
by Tony G—

Long, long ago all the magic was beneath the sea. Once upon a time there was a sea monster named Ben, who was light green and very big. One day he ate two magical fish who were also green. Then he became magical too. The magical sea monster's family was very happy because now their son was magical.

Part of the sea monster's magic was that he could turn into different colors like brown. He could also turn fish into smaller things and get a bigger meal and not have to take such big bites. The sea monster's family was very happy because now they could eat whatever they wanted to. They were glad until their son was bitten by another sea monster. Then Ben's family was very sad.

Now the other sea monster had the magic. His name was Spencer. Ben died from the bite and got camouflaged and he fell to the bottom of the ocean. He looked like the sand. Soon Spencer the sea monster got eaten by another sea monster and then that monster got the magic.

After a very long time, the humans found out about the magic below the sea. Soon they built a submarine. They sent it off to get the magic and soon they found what they wanted. Below them they saw a magical sea monster trying to catch a fish.

The humans saw the magical sea monster and they fired an enormous ship that took the magic from the sea monster. Then the magical sea monster died. The humans took the magic into their ship and brought it back to land. The humans used the magic to learn things about the ocean.

There were still more sea monsters in the ocean, but none of them were magical. They had to find magical fish to eat first.

Now there was magic above the sea and below the sea.

Artifact #9

Perspectives

An elementary school counselor realizes that children often have only a limited ability to look at the world from other people's perspectives. To foster greater perspective taking, she has developed a series of activities for third, fourth, and fifth graders. On the following page, she describes the activities.

Questions to Consider as You Examine the Activities

- How does perspective-taking ability change with age? Characterize the typical perspective-taking ability of children in the upper elementary school grades. (Look in your educational psychology or child development textbook for answers to these questions.)

- Identify the specific things that children might learn from the activities. What kinds of perspective taking do they entail? What kinds of perspective taking do they *not* entail?

- Considering what you know about learning and cognitive development, speculate about how effective the counselor's activities are likely to be in fostering greater perspective taking.

- What other kinds of activities might a teacher or counselor conduct to foster perspective taking?

UNDERSTANDING DIFFERENT PERSPECTIVES

Read to the class the book, <u>Just Another Ordinary Day</u> [R. Clement, HarperCollins, 1997]. Have them close their eyes and picture the scenes mentally. Then show the children the actual pictures. Ask the children if they "saw" the pictures differently.

Ask the children what the word PERSPECTIVE means. Wave your hand in front of the class and ask them what you are doing. (waving goodbye, waving hello, washing a window, waving for help, etc.)

Put a variety of objects in a box. Without looking, have children feel what is in the box and guess what it is. Ask the children WHY they guessed what they did. (past experiences)

Play "Telephone" and have the children experience how everyone has a different experience and interpretation of the same thing. Talk about why and how our past experiences change how we "look" at things. Discuss how rumors start this way, and the importance of "going to the source."

Artifact #10

Self-Reflection #1

At the end of his third-grade year, 9-year-old Andrew evaluates his progress in various academic subjects, as well as in work habits and social skills. His "self-progress report" appears on the following page.

Questions to Consider as You Examine the Report

- What does the report reveal about Andrew's general self-concept and self-esteem, as well as about his self-efficacy for various tasks?

- How insightful is Andrew about his strengths and weaknesses? What kinds of qualities and behaviors does he focus on? What things does he tend to overlook?

- What are the benefits of completing such a report? In identifying benefits, draw on what you have learned about motivation, cognition, and self-regulation.

- Compare this writing sample at age 9 to Andrew's book report (Artifact #4) at age 7. What improvements do you see?

- Compare Andrew's self-reflection with that of 12-year-old Landra (Artifact #16). What developmental differences do you see? Relate these differences to what you have learned about cognitive and personal development.

<u>June Self-Progress Report</u>

READING I am able to read more books, read longer books. i have fun reading.

WRITING i can spell more words. write more and write neater.

MATH better at times, and reading clok's and grafs.

SCIENCE/SOCIAL STUDIES I like eletricity because I like to use it.

WORK HABITS I can work faster and better.

SOCIAL BEHAVIOR I talk at work times.

Comments about my year in third grade. I went on field trips of and have more friends.

Artifact #11

Snow

A fourth-grade class is studying strategies for descriptive writing. In one lesson, the teacher asks students to pick a particular object or event and brainstorm ways of describing it using five different sensory modalities: feeling, tasting, looking, smelling, and hearing. Students then draw on their brainstormed ideas to write a rough draft of a descriptive composition. The following day, they edit their rough drafts and create a final, polished piece. Ten-year-old Shea uses these three steps to write a description of snow, as shown on the following three pages.

Questions to Consider as You Examine the Brainstorming Sheet and Two Drafts

- What are the advantages of breaking a creative writing task into such steps? In identifying advantages, draw on what you have learned about cognition and memory.

- In what ways does Shea edit her rough draft? In what ways does she *not* edit it?

- In what ways has the teacher apparently scaffolded the writing task?

Snow

(Sometimes smooth, sometimes lumpy)
(hard to drive in), makes everything
look beautiful, soft, or wonderful to
play in, day off from school, time with
friends, snowball fights, injuries, fun
with dad, hot chocolate after playing
in it, very wet, not always fun, cause
accidents, make

feel ✓
taste ✓
look ✓
smell ✓
hear ✓

Snow

Snow makes everything look like a fairy kingdom in the winter. Snow ~~something~~ *sometimes* looks as smooth as a ~~desktop~~, sometimes snow looks as lumpy as a pillow after a pillow fight. # Snow is as soft as a cloud, and is just as wet as a cloud ~~properly is~~ *one*. # Snow does not taste very good, but the hot chocolate you get after playing in it does. # Snow does ~~not~~ *taste good* have a smell when it is alone. When it is by pinetrees ~~thoug~~ it absorbes their fresh smeel # ~~Snow does not sound~~ like anything, nether does ~~season~~ winter. This how I decribe snow useing ~~my~~ five of my ~~senses~~ *scences*.

Decribing Snow

Snow makes everything look like a fairy kingdom in the winter. Snow sometimes looks as smooth as a desktop; sometimes snow looks as lumpy as a pillow after a pillow fight.

Snow is as soft as a cloud and just as wet as one.

Snow does not taste very good, but the hot chocolate you get after playing in it does taste good.

Snow does not have a smell when it is alone. When it is by pinetrees it absorbes their fresh smell.

Snow does not sound like anything nether does the season winter. This is how decribe snow useing five of my seénces.

Artifact #12

Watercolor Rubric

A fourth-grade art class is learning techniques for painting with watercolor paints. The final project for the unit is to complete a watercolor collage. The art teacher creates a rubric to evaluate the students' collages and uses it to communicate with parents about their children's performance on the project. The rubric, filled out for a boy named Connor, appears on the following page.

Questions to Consider as You Examine the Rubric

- What qualities of the student's performance does the rubric identify?

- What are the rubric's strengths? What are its shortcomings?

- How might you improve the rubric?

- What inferences might Connor's parents draw from the information presented?

WATERCOLOR COLLAGE

_____Connor_____ has completed a watercolor collage. This was a two step project that began with a watercolor experiment sheet. After we talked about the qualities of the water paint media and a short demonstration of technique variations, the students each explored the properties and possibilities of watercolor. For the most part these pages were very nice works in themselves but we made them even more exciting when we cut them up and arranged them on colored construction paper. A worksheet became art.

Rubric: 5=outstanding, 4=Very strong, 3=Equal balance of strengths and weaknesses, 2=Needs Improvement, 1=Incomplete

Arrangement of pieces shows thoughtful planning _3_____

Care was used in cutting and glueing _2_____

Finished piece is interesting and powerful _3-_____

I don't get the feeling that Connor was concentrating very hard on this.

Artifact #13

Spelling Test

Nine-year-old Jason attends fourth grade at a small private school that routinely individualizes assignments to accommodate students' strengths and weaknesses; hence, teachers rarely refer students to be evaluated for possible disabilities. Throughout his school career, Jason has shown many signs of giftedness (e.g., an ability to learn quickly, early emergence of abstract thinking, strong social and leadership skills). However, Jason consistently exhibits difficulties with written language. As an example, his performance on a weekly spelling test appears on the next page.

Questions to Consider as You Examine the Spelling Test

- What words is Jason trying to spell?

- What aspects of written language has Jason mastered? What aspects has he *not* mastered?

- Judging from what you have previously observed about fourth graders, is Jason's performance typical for his grade level? If not, what aspects of his performance are unusual for students at his grade level?

- Do you think Jason has a disability? If so, what might it be?

- If Jason has a disability, what would be the advantages of having it identified as such? What might be potential disadvantages?

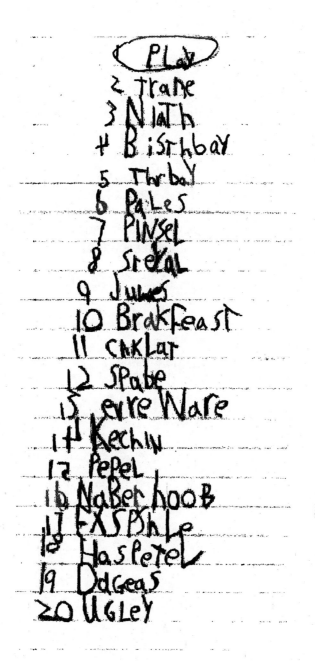

1 PLaY

2 TraNe

3 NiaTh

4 BiSThbaY

5 ThrbaY

6 PaLes

7 PiNSeL

8 SreaL

9 JuNes

10 BrakFeaST

11 CNKLar

12 SPabe

13 evre Ware

14 Kechiv

15 PePeL

16 NaBerhooB

17 EXSPShLe

18 HaSPeTeL

19 DdGeaS

20 UGLeY

Artifact #14

New Year's Resolutions

In January of 1999, students in a fifth-grade class in Bexley, Ohio, write papers describing their resolutions for the new year. The second draft of 10-year-old Shannon's paper appears on the following two pages.

Questions to Consider as You Examine the Paper

- What benefits might such a goal-setting activity have for students? In answering this question, draw on what you have learned about motivation and/or the development of self-regulation.

- Are Shannon's goals for herself realistic? Why or why not?

- What does Shannon's final goal tell us about her personal, social, and/or moral development?

- What strategies might a teacher use to help Shannon follow through on working to meet her goals?

Draft I

One of my new year's resolutions is to do my back exercises every day. So I don't end up wearing a brace. If I did end up wearing a back brace I'd have to do back exercises anyway. Why do 2 insted of 1? I made this resolution on January 1, 1997 and haven't broken it yet!

Another one of my resolutions is to proofread <u>all</u> of my work. So I don't make as many careless mistakes. I know that I leave out words sometimes in my writing pieces and which makes them harder to read. And in other subjects I make mistakes that wouldn't make if I would proofread.

My next resolution is to practice my clarinet for 100 minutes a week. So on Monday, Wednesday, Friday, and Sunday I practice my clarinet

for 20 to 30 minutes.
My last new year's goal
is probably the most important.
My goal is to help my fourth grade
friend who doesn't go to school in
Bexley study for the Ohio Fourth
Profincieny Test. You see my friend
class really fell behind. I am helping
my friend build up her knowledge
and her confidence. So what if it
doesn't help me get good posture,
good grades, or help me get good at
playing the clarinet. It helps both
my friend and me feel good.

Artifact #15

A Really Bad Day

For a district-wide writing assessment, the public schools of the Commonwealth of the Northern Mariana Islands (located north of Guam in the Pacific Ocean) ask fifth graders to write about one of three topics. One boy chooses the topic "Gosh, yesterday was a really bad day!" His narrative appears on the following page.

Questions to Consider as You Examine the Writing Sample

- What strengths do you see in the boy's writing? What areas need improvement?

- Do you think the narrative is nonfiction or fiction? Draw on elements of the story and your own prior knowledge to support your decision.

- What things do you know or might you infer about the boy's family life?

- To what extent do you think the narrative accurately depicts the boy's typical behavior at school? Explain your reasoning.

When I woke up for
school and went to shower but
I can't shower because of my
Dad taking his sweet time.
After 15 minutes in the bath-
room. I went to go get dresst
up for school. Luckilly I was
5 minutes early. I could'nt
eat breakfast because I owed
the lunch lady seven dollars
and fifty cents. Then the
bell rang for class. I ran
to class and I forgot my
home work at the car. When
my friend Kyle talked to
me. I kept talking to him.
Me and Kyle talked about

Men in tights that was
about robbin hood and his
gang. My teacher saw us talking
and scolded me and kyle.
My teacher gave us a warning.
Me and kyle did'nt care
we thought Mr. would give
us a nother chance to me
and kyle. So we kept talking
and talking not paying
atention to our work. Me
and kyle got all wrongs in
our math exercise. After
school my teacher talked to
me and called up my parents
My parents scolded me and
grounded me for 3 weeks plus
because of Eavedroping
on the phone when my sister
is talking to her boyfriend.

Artifact #16

Self-Reflection #2

As part of a "life skills" course during the fall of her sixth-grade year, 12-year-old Landra writes an essay describing her strengths and weaknesses. Her essay appears on the following page.

Questions to Consider as You Examine the Essay

- What does the report reveal about Landra's general self-concept and self-esteem, as well as about her self-efficacy for various tasks?

- How insightful is Landra about her strengths and weaknesses? What kinds of qualities and behaviors does she focus on? What things does she tend to overlook?

- What are the benefits of writing such an essay? In identifying benefits, draw on what you have learned about motivation, personal development, and self-regulation.

- Compare Landra's self-reflection with that of 9-year-old Andrew (Artifact #10). What developmental differences do you see? Relate these differences to what you have learned about cognitive and personal development.

My strengths mostly have to do with people. I love to hang out with my friends, "socialize" or talk, and work with people. I feel really comfortable talking to people and meeting new people. I think that being very people smart has helped me out in the first weeks of 6th grade and will throughout the rest of my life because I am going to be meeting new people all the time. Some other strengths of mine are music, self, and body smart. I am very aware of what is good and bad for me. I play tennis three times a week, do ballet and jazz dance, and run. I eat healthy foods so I consider myself body smart. I have high self-esteem, too. I love listening to CDs and the radio. However, I can't read notes that well. I played the piano for about two months and then I quit. Taking choir is helping me learn the notes and hopefully I will understand them. Also, I am pretty good at spelling and writing, but I wouldn't want to write for a living. I enjoy math, but it is not my favorite subject. It's not my weakness, but it's not my strength either. I enjoy drawing and designing a lot! I might want to be a fashion designer or landscape architect for my career.

My number one weakness, though, is nature! Taking nature walks and being in the dark woods at night aren't my favorite things to do. However, I do like the woods in October because the leaves are so beautiful. In terms of finding my way in the woods, on a scale of 1-10 I would get a 3 at the most because I have basically no idea how a compass works. So those are my strengths, weaknesses, and smarts.

Artifact #17

Trees

When beginning a unit on trees, a sixth-grade science teacher asks students to open their class journals to the first blank page and write down all the things they can think of that they know about trees. Once the students have completed their lists, the teacher asks them to turn to the next page and write the things they *don't* know about trees but would like to learn—in other words, to list questions they have about trees. Later, as the class proceeds through the tree unit, the teacher encourages the students to take notes on the new things they learn about trees.

The entries in one student's journal appear on the next three pages. As you will see, they are titled, "What I Know about trees," "Questions I have," and "What I Learned." The teacher's reactions appear in smaller cursive, typically toward the right-hand side of the pages.

Questions to Consider as You Examine the Journal Entries

- How might listing what they already know about trees help the students learn new things?

- What benefits might listing questions about trees have for learning?

- Look at the notes on the page "What I Learned." What are some possible explanations for the brevity of the notes?

- How effective are the teacher's comments?

- What strategies might a teacher use to help the students take more complete and informative notes?

What I Know
about trees

- in the plant Kingdom
- they are green
- in the fall trees leave cange color and fall off
- trees are living things
- trees probace seeds
- trees photosyntheis
- leaves are diffent shapes and sizes
- trees have roots
- trees take n CO_2

good

Questions I have

- What tells the trees to change color
- Are there and "trees" under-water? some the roots are like mangrove forests
- What makes leaves diffent colors?
- How many leaves does the avrage tree have?
- where is the biggest tree in the world?
- Is sea weed considered a "tree"? no an algae/protists

- Do evergreen trees change color like oll trees?

- How fast do trees goron?

- What is the smallest full grown tree?

- Is there one tree with only one of its kind

- Is there any kind of way to tell when a ginco tree will those its leaves (frost)

good questions
Very impressive

What I Learned

good start

- chlorophil is the green pigment in a leaf that make it green.
- carotenes is the orange pigment in a leaf

Artifact #18

Friends

As an assignment for a unit on "relationships" in one of her middle school classes, 12-year-old Grace completes a questionnaire about friends and friendship. The questionnaire and Grace's responses appear on the next two pages.

Questions to Consider as You Examine the Questionnaire

- What purposes might the questionnaire serve? What benefits might it have for students? What benefits might it have for teachers and other school personnel?

- What roles do friends appear to serve in Grace's life? Relate your response to what you have learned about personal and social development more generally.

- What social skills does Grace appear to have?

- As you might be able to tell from her responses, Grace is a sociable sixth grader with many friends. How might a "loner" respond to various items on the questionnaire? How might an especially aggressive student respond to the items?

Friendship Questions
Points: 15

Name:_____

Period:_____

1. List three qualities you look for in a friend:

    a. trustworthiness

    b. funny & nice

    c. caring

2. List three qualities you would **not** want in a friend:

    a. untrustworthy

    b. mean

    c. unfair

3. Friends are important to me because...

they make me laugh, make me feel better, listen to me, give me an alternative to my parents (to talk to) because they REALLY understand.

4. To be a good friend, I should...

Try to do all of the things I look for in a friend & be myself.

5. It is hard to make new friends sometimes because...

They don't want or like you or you don't like them. Sometimes people jump to conclusions by supposing or judging someone they don't even know.

6. Some ways to make new friends are...

to be openminded. Think of the other side of the story: their point of view on you. Make a good 1st impression.

7. Write a paragraph describing the kind of friend you are:

I think that I'm a really good friend. People can count on me & I'm responsible. My best quality is that I'm a very good listener. I'm very down to earth (serious) but I can also be wild (fun). Of course, I'm not perfect so I do have a few not so good qualities. I try not to take sides, but I sometimes do.

8. Write a paragraph describing someone you would like to be friends with:

This pretty much describes my best, best friend! Maggie I've known Maggie since I was 4 years old. We share secrets & she keeps them. We laugh together & act stupid together & we're serious together. She has a good balance of the 6 pillars of ethical behavior and that's what I look for.

9. Describe what you would do in the following situations:

a. When Laura tells Jessica something private, Jessica passes the information along to others. If you were Laura, what would you do?

I'd probably 1st get mad at her then tell her how I felt. I wouldn't trust her for a while.

b. Drake listens to all of Marty's complaints, but Marty will never take the time to listen to him. What can Drake do?

Tell him how he feels, give him 1 more chance, and if that doesn't work, go to someone else.

c. Tonya doesn't want Stacey to have any other friends but her. How can Stacey handle this problem?

Tell Tonya that she is allowed to have other friends besides her. I'd be open with her & give her a chance to meet the other people. If she doesn't fit in then she should try harder.

Artifact #19

Clifford's Tower

Year 7 (seventh grade) students attending Harrogate Grammar School in North Yorkshire, England, are on a field trip to Clifford's Tower, an old fortress in York. The teacher, Darrell Harris, has given his students an eight-page handout (created by his colleague Helen Snelson) to guide them as they explore the tower in small work groups. Appearing on the first page of the handout is the following "key question" that the students should be able to answer at the end of the field trip:

> **KEY QUESTION:**
>
> *Why was Clifford's Tower built?*

The students begin their exploration by studying the outside of the tower (known in medieval days as a *keep*) and then proceed to the inside, where they examine the tower's features and displays. The handout presents numerous questions that the students should answer during their tour. Although the students work in small groups, they must each answer these questions on their own individual copies of the handout.

Four pages from the handout appear on the following two pages. (English Heritage, mentioned in question 11, is the organization that maintains Clifford's Tower.)

Questions to Consider as You Examine the Handout

- Speculate about the teacher's objectives for the field trip.

- To what extent do the questions focus on lower-level versus higher-level skills? Which questions might be especially effective in promoting effective learning and memory processes?

- On the surface, the handout is designed to guide the students as they learn about Clifford's Tower. Yet it may also help them construct more sophisticated views about the *nature of historical thinking* (in other words, more sophisticated epistemological beliefs). In what ways does the handout encourage students to think about historical edifices and events?

- Why do you think the teacher has the students work in small groups yet respond to the handout's questions individually?

HAVE A GOOD LOOK AT THE SMALL HILL (THE MOTTE) ON WHICH CLIFFORD'S TOWER IS STOOD.

The motte is 13m high, about 68m in diameter at the bottom and about 30m in diameter at the top. It was once surrounded by a moat, filled with water from the River Foss.

3 Do you think the motte is natural or man-made?

4 Why do you think this?

5 Why do you think the Tower (known as the keep) was put on a motte?

READ THIS!

In 1069, just one year after the castle was built, the Danes invaded and the people of York supported them against William. York was set on fire and the castles destroyed. William was so angry he burnt and destroyed the whole area. It is called 'The Harrying of the North'. He rebuilt the castle too!

DO THE NEXT SECTION OF WORK INSIDE THE KEEP

DO THIS WORK AT THE BOTTOM OF THE TOWER

READ THIS!

In October 1066, William the Conqueror beat King Harold Godwineson at the Battle of Hastings in the south of England. He became king, but he did not have control of the north. He marched north in 1068 and set up a wooden castle in York on this site. William or one of his rich supporters could live in the castle with soldiers and 'keep an eye' on the locals.

STUDY THE MAP OF MEDIEVAL YORK TO THE LEFT OF THIS BOX

1 Suggest why William built his castle here? (Clue: think about defence and remember that rivers were important for transport.)

STUDY THE DIAGRAM OF THE MOTTE AND BAILEY CASTLE

2 Circle the part of the York motte and bailey castle that still exists today.

11 How do English Heritage know that the upper floor was used as a living area?

12 Think about all the comforts you have at home. Only the richest medieval people would have lived in a castle. Suggest how or where these rich people:

- heated the castle

- made it light when it was dark

- got their water from

- cooked their food

- went to the toilet

- were protected from danger

Find this information on the display boards:

6 When was the keep rebuilt in stone?

AMAZING FACTS!
1 The walls are 3 metres thick!
2 A French castle inspired the design for Clifford's Tower!

LOOK CAREFULLY AT THE INSIDE OF THE TOWER AND THINK HARD!

7 Make a list of the features which make the tower easy to defend.

> Did you know, stone towers are more expensive to build, but are stronger than wooden towers?

8 What evidence can you see that there were problems when this heavy stone building was built on the motte?

9 What evidence can you see that there was an upper floor to this building?

10 What evidence tells us that there was once a roof on this building?

51

Artifact #20

Taking Notes

As they begin a unit on Greek mythology, a seventh-grade language arts teacher gives each of her students several copies of a "Story Note Taking Form" that they should use as they take notes on each of the myths they will be studying. She also distributes a handout that offers several hints about how to take notes effectively. The form and handout appear on the next two pages.

Questions to Consider as You Examine the Form and Handout

- Are the form and handout developmentally appropriate for seventh graders? Justify your answer based on what you have learned about the typical learning strategies and metacognitive development of 12- and 13-year-olds.

- What strengths do you see in the "Note Taking Hints" handout?

- How might you improve the handout?

- How might you change the note-taking form so that it would be appropriate for a science class? for a math class? for a social studies class?

Story Note Taking Form

Title:_____

Author:_____

I.   Characters (write a few notes after each character's name to describe them, make an abbreviation after the character's name for further notes)

    a. _____

    b. _____

    c. _____

    d. _____

    e. _____

    f. _____

    g. _____

    h. _____

II. Setting (write a few notes after the place to describe it, try to discover the time period)

    a. _____

    b. _____

    c. _____

III. Events

    a. _____

    b. _____

    c. _____

    d. _____

    e. _____

    f. _____

IV. Conflict (what is the problem, who is involved)

    a. _____

    b. _____

V.   Solution (how did the problem work itself out, was there a lesson to learn)

    a. _____

    b. _____

Note Taking Hints

I. Listen 80%, write 20%

    a. Note taking is trying to pick out the important information, so listen for what's important.

    b. Phrases that indicate importance:
        1. "The main points are..."
        2. "The four characteristics of..."
        3. "The two causes are..."
        4. "These four reasons are..."

    c. We listen by:
        1. Resisting distractions
        2. Clarifying to ourselves what is being said
        3. Paying attention to speaker cues (voice, physical cues, rate of speech)
        4. Writing what is important

II. Invent your own shorthand

    a. Shorten words that you use often (with = w/, because = b/c, and = +)

    b. Make a "shorthand key" when you are done (Per = Persephone)

III. Know what you are taking notes from and make subtopics

    a. Notes from a story will have the following subtopics:
        1. Character, setting, problem, solution/lesson

    b. Notes from a textbook will have the topic and its details
        1. You can find the subtopics by looking at the bold print

Artifact #21

Math Quiz

A seventh-grade math teacher wants to find out what her students have learned about fractions, decimals, and percentages. She constructs a brief quiz that will take little class time and be easy to score. The quiz has three parts:

1. Students must determine whether two numbers in each of six pairs are equal or unequal and use the appropriate sign (>, <, or =) to indicate how one number in the pair compares to the other.

2. Students must convert fractions and percentages to decimals.

3. Students must determine whether two numbers in each of six pairs are equal and answer either "true" (for equal numbers) or "false" (for unequal numbers).

A copy of the quiz, with one student's answers and the teacher's feedback, appears on the following page.

Questions to Consider as You Examine the Quiz

- Speculate about the extent to which the quiz is a *reliable* measure of what the students have learned.

- What additional information would you need to have in order to determine whether the quiz has high *validity* in this situation?

- What kinds of instructional objectives does the quiz reflect?

- What message does the quiz give about the *nature of mathematics as a discipline*?

- What kinds of test items might you construct if you wanted to assess students' ability to apply their knowledge of fractions, decimals, and percentages to real-world situations?

Compare these numbers. Use $>$, $<$, $=$

1. 7 $\gt$ 3
2. $\frac{9}{10}$ $\lt$ $\frac{10}{9}$
3. 19.6 $\gt$ 19.061
4. 11 $\lt$ 11^2
5. 209 $\gt$ 29.0
6. 1^3 $=$ 1^2

Change to decimals

7. $\frac{3}{5}$ = 0.6 ✓
8. 75% = 0.75 ✓
9. $\frac{2}{11}$ = 0.22
10. 47% = 0.47 ✓
11. $\frac{7}{2}$ = 3.5
12. $3\frac{1}{4}$ = 3.25 ✓
13. $\frac{3}{10}$ = 0.3 ✓
14. $\frac{17}{8}$ = 2.125 ✓

True or False

15. $\frac{1}{2}$ = $\frac{11}{22}$ True ✓
16. 3.2 = $\frac{17}{5}$ False ✓
17. $2\frac{1}{5}$ = 2.3   True
18. $\frac{19}{20}$ = 95%   True ✓
19. $\frac{16}{6}$ = $\frac{40}{15}$ False
20. $\frac{6}{7}$ = 0.67   False ✓

Artifact #22

Variables

In her seventh-grade science class, Jalila has completed an activity at a classroom "station," where she learned about variables in scientific research. She learned that a *variable* is any characteristic or condition in the research situation that may vary. She also learned about three kinds of variables in a scientific investigation:

- An *independent variable* is one that the researcher manipulates to determine its effect on something else.

- A *dependent variable* is one that the researcher measures to determine whether it changes as a result of the independent variable. It is the "something else" that, in the researcher's hypothesis, an independent variable might influence.

- A *controlled variable* is one that the researcher tries to keep constant during the course of the investigation. Ideally, the researcher wants to hold constant all variables in the research situation except for the independent and dependent variables. In this way, the researcher can better determine whether a cause-and-effect relationship exists between the independent and dependent variables being studied.

At home that night, Jalila writes a reaction paper describing what she has learned during the activity. Her paper appears on the following page.

Questions to Consider as You Examine the Paper

- With regard to Jalila's *writing*, what strengths and weaknesses do you see?

- What things from the lesson has Jalila learned accurately? What limitations do you see in her understanding of variables and the scientific method?

- What evidence do you see that Jalila has learned some parts of the lesson in a meaningful fashion? What evidence do you see that she has learned some parts only at a rote level?

- What things might Jalila have included in her paper to show that she truly understands the nature of variables in scientific inquiry?

- Most seventh graders are 12 or 13 years old. Given what you know about cognitive development, is the lesson appropriate for seventh graders? Why or why not?

I learned a lot from the variables station. I learned that a variable is something that changes. There are three types of variables. One is an independent variable (also known as a manipulated variable) and it is something that is purposely changed by the investigator. The independent variable is the "cause" in the cause and effect relationship. The second type of variable is the responding or dependent variable, which is affected by the change that has been made. It is the "effect" in the cause and effect relationship. Finally the third, is the controlling variable that never changes. It always stays the same.

I do think that variables are important. Why? Because they are the basics of each experiment. Without the variables in a scientific experiment, we would have no idea what happened before and after and what changes were made. If we don't know that then we might make the same mistake all over again and that would be a waste of time. Come to think of it, without variables there wouldn't be the 2nd and 4th step in the scientific method: the hypothesis (cause) and the conclusion (effect). So variables are extremely important.

I am glad that I know about variables. I found out the scientific name for "change" and "cause and effect". Mostly I learned a lot.

Artifact #23

Holocaust Museum

Three weeks before they take a 4-day field trip to Washington, D.C., eighth graders at an Ohio middle school are each assigned a particular Washington landmark, institution, or museum in which they will "specialize." They have two weeks to learn about their assigned site, write a detailed description, and create and illustrate a brochure that would be appropriate for visitors to the site. Later, when the class is in Washington, the students distribute their brochures to their classmates and act as tour guides, using the bus microphone to tell their fellow passengers about their site's history, characteristics, and special features.

As an example, 14-year-old Grace focuses on the U.S. Holocaust Memorial Museum. Her brochure appears on the next two pages. On the brochure itself, the two pages are printed back-to-back; the brochure is then folded vertically into thirds. As you will notice, Grace puts the title of the brochure on the same side of the page as the final column of text so that after the brochure is folded the various parts will be sequenced appropriately.

Questions to Consider as You Examine the Brochure

- Consider both the brochure and the "tour guide" activity described above. What benefits might these assignments have? In identifying the benefits, draw on what you have learned about learning and motivation.

- What kinds of scaffolding might a teacher need to provide to help students develop good presentations and brochures?

General Information

President Jimmy Carter proposed the idea for the museum on September 27, 1979. Construction began on October 1, 1980 and was opened on April 22, 1993 by President Bill Clinton. Everyday, 5,000 people go through the museum. There are 5 floors and visitors work their ways down from the 4th Floor to the Concourse Level. There are both permanent and temporary exhibits in the US Holocaust Memorial Museum.

Other Exhibits

There are two main permanent exhibits to see. One is made for kids, called Daniel's Story. This exhibit is about a young boy, named

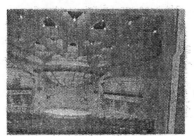

Daniel, and his journey through the concentration camps and his persecution. It is suitable for children 8 years and older.

The other, more popular exhibit is called "The Holocaust". This exhibit gives visitors a more in-depth view of what really happened during that awful time. There are interactive stations with TV monitors, "gas chambers", a walk-through railcar, a much more. This is a rather graphic and emotionally disturbing exhibit and is recommended for visitors 11 and up.

What's in the Museum?

There are thousands of artifacts in the Holocaust Museum. Some are 2500 photos, 1000 real artifacts, 53 video monitors, and 30 interactive studios containing graphic and emotionally disturbing images of violence. There are also shoes, eating utensils, hair shaven form inmates at Auschwitz, and a violin used to entertain Nazis at private parties.

The Tours

All tours begin on the top floor, the 4th Floor. This floor contains information documenting the early years of the Nazi Regime and the beginning of the persecution of Jews. Working your way down to the 3rd Floor, it has exhibits pertaining to the "Final Solution", also known as putting undesirables in concentration camps and killing 6 million of them. The

2nd Floor is the home of the Hall of Witnesses, which holds the names of those persecuted and killed. In the Hall of Remembrance is the Eternal Flame, lit by President Clinton, Nobel Laurete Elie Weisel and Harvey M. Meyerhoff on April 22, 1993. The 1st Floor currently holds the Hall of Witnesses and other rotating temporary exhibits. Lastly, the tour ends on the Concourse Level, which contains the Children's Tile Wall. This wall has 100's of tiles painted by children commemorating the 1.5 million children murdered during the Holocaust.

WHERE IS IT?
1000 Raoul Wallenberg Place, SW.
Washington DC, 20024

www.ushmm.org

The United States Holocaust Memorial Museum

Artifact #24

The Three A's

A ninth-grade class spends a class period learning "Three A's" for school success: attitude, activity, and accountability. One student's notes from the class appear on the following page.

Questions to Consider as You Examine the Notes

- Look at the bullets that the student has written. To what extent does each bullet allow you to infer the ideas that the teacher presented? More generally, how effectively will the notes help the student recall the content of the class?

- In which bullets do you find the following concepts reflected?
  - Metacognition
  - Self-regulation
  - Motivation

- What other concepts related to learning, motivation, and/or development do you see reflected in the bullets?

- How effective do you think such a lesson might be? What are its potential benefits? What are its potential weaknesses?

3 A's

Attitude

- am I on time?
- do I ~~have~~ talk positively about doing well in school?
- do I manage my time well
- do I associate with successful friends
- do I have an A student attitude?
- change perspective
- Is extra help geeky?
- Are my teachers my ~~adversaries~~ enemies or my collaboraters?
- what's more important, being accepted or my goals?
- watch your self-talk
  - ~ I'm just an accelerated student

Activity

- Don't do just enough school or homework ^to just get by and ~~be~~ miserable
- Determine at 2:30 what needs to be done and when
- Do the little things
- Do I have enough down time?
- Routines
- Have assignments all in one place
- Find a mentor (role-model)

Accountability

- Average people are accountable to ~~others;~~ successful people are accountable to themselves
- examine habits and tweak them to achieve ~~your~~ my goals
- Some rely on feelings to get things done

How should I do this?

- Take something I like
- ~~You~~ Eliminate ~~an~~ it until my priority is done

63

Artifact #25

Dark Magic

As an assignment for his high school English class, 14-year-old Geoff has written an essay comparing J. K. Rowling's *Harry Potter and the Sorcerer's Stone* and J. R. R. Tolkien's *The Fellowship of the Ring*. Geoff's essay and his teacher's evaluation appear on the next four pages.

Questions to Consider as You Examine the Essay and Evaluation Form

- What are the advantages of the assignment the teacher has given? What challenges might students face as they complete the assignment?

- Geoff intentionally puts some of his sentences in boldface. Speculate on what he is using boldface print for.

- Early in the school year, the teacher has given students a copy of the checklist he is now using to evaluate Geoff's paper. What are the advantages of such a checklist?

- How thorough is the checklist? Are there additional things you might add to it?

Dark Magic Through the Ages

Harry Potter and the Sorcerer's Stone and The Fellowship of the Ring are both modern classics in the eyes of many readers. They both contain a struggle between good and evil and magical lands filled with magical creatures. Some of these creatures are good and some are evil. The evil creatures use magic, known as dark magic, for their own evil deeds such as destroying the innocent and good willed. Their failure to use their dark magic correctly leads to a long tale of good versus evil. **In Harry Potter and the Sorcerer's Stone and The Fellowship of the Ring, the conflict of the story is initiated by the use of dark magic in order to destroy a living being; in Harry Potter, Voldemort, is trying to destroy Harry, while in Fellowship of the Ring, Sauron, is trying to destroy many kinds of living beings, such as hobbits, men and elves.**

In Harry Potter and the Sorcerer's Stone, Voldemort tries to kill Harry but fails; as a result, the conflict of the story is initiated by the use of dark magic. Voldemort killed Harry's parents first and then killed Harry. Harry tells Dumbledore, *"Voldemort said he only killed my mother because she tried to stop him from killing me"* (371). This explains that Voldemort's purpose was to kill Harry (for some unknown reason) and it is likely he will come back. Shortly after Harry was attacked, many wizards celebrating Voldemort's defeat talked about his attack; even Professor McGonagall heard. Professor McGonagall told Dumbledore, *"They're saying he tried to kill the Potters son, Harry"* (15). All the wizards in the world were celebrating Voldemort's defeat. Voldemort had lost his powers so, of course, he would desire revenge. Hagrid informed Harry of his attack when he was picking him up to go to Hogwarts. Hagrid explains to Harry, *"You-*

Know-Who killed 'em. And then... he tried to kill you" (<u>64</u>). Hagrid is explaining the importance of what happened to Harry as a baby and tells of Voldemort's dark powers. Harry finds out he's famous at this time.

In the <u>Fellowship of the Ring</u>, Sauron makes a ring to destroy many kinds of living beings but fails; as a result, the conflict of the story is initiated by the use of dark magic. Gandalf comes to visit Frodo once he finds out about the dangers of the Ring. <u>Gandalf tells Frodo</u>, "*...if he often uses the Ring to make himself invisible, he fades... and walks in the twilight under the eye of the dark power that rules the Rings*" (<u>51</u>). Gandalf is explaining the power of the Ring to Frodo in the passage and that the Ring has only one master that will always control it. Gandalf goes on to tell him what the Ring says. <u>The Ring says</u>, "*One Ring to rule them all, One Ring to find them, One Ring to bring them all and in the darkness bind them*" (<u>55</u>). Gandalf not only proves that this is the One Ring but shows how much power Sauron has over it and it's power. Gandalf goes on to tell more of what Sauron has in store. <u>Gandalf explains to Frodo</u>, "*The Enemy still lacks one thing to give him strength and knowledge to beat down all resistance. He lacks the One Ring*" (<u>56</u>). Gandalf explain to Frodo Sauron's plan and exactly the power and deadliness of the Ring.

The two evil characters in the stories use dark magic to eliminate a being or beings but fail; as a result, end up initiating the conflict of the story. Fantasy writers have used the use of both good versus evil and magic for centuries. Magic has been used to transport the reader to a place, and maybe time, where he or she has never been and possibly never will be. Both stories have a large fan base and have, and always will, influence later writers.

(90) Well-done, Geoff! You followed the format very well.
I would work on a) S.S.
b) verb quality

Mr. Pawlyk's Thesis Paper Checklist *(in order of priority)*

This checklist should be used for the composition of any formal academic essays between 2-3 pages. For longer essays, the lengths below may change but the structural principles remain the same. Although teachers differ on the subtleties of form, this little sheet will help you eliminate many needless errors as well as help structure your argument more clearly, effectively, and persuasively.

I.   The Thesis Statement

1) 1 sentence that concludes the introduction
2) titles of the text(s) given
3) specific fact about the topic is linked to its relevance to the entire text
4) is based on an objective (not subjective) response
5) assertive in tone / no 1st person used ("I feel, I think," etc.)

good

[Note: If your thesis does not meet the above criteria, do not move on . . .you'll just waste time].

II.   Body Paragraph 1

1) 1st sentence is a topic sentence linking the body paragraph to the thesis
2) 1-2 context sentences setting the reader up for the quotation
3) introduction to quotation (speaker and comma), quotation, page # in parenthesis
4) 1-2 supporting sentences (linking the previous quotation to the topic sentence above)   X need to be stronger
5) repeat #2-4 for 1 or 2 more quotations
6) concluding sentence

III.   Body Paragraph 2

1) 1st sentence is a topic sentence linking the body paragraph to the thesis
2) 1-2 context sentences setting the reader up for the quotation
3) introduction to quotation (speaker and comma), quotation, page # in parenthesis
4) 1-2 supporting sentences (linking the previous quotation to the topic sentence above)   X
5) repeat #2-4 for 1 or 2 more quotations
6) concluding sentence

IV.   Body Paragraph 3 (if necessary)

1) 1st sentence is a topic sentence linking the body paragraph to the thesis
2) 1-2 context sentences setting the reader up for the quotation
3) introduction to quotation (speaker and comma), quotation, page # in parenthesis
4) 1-2 supporting sentences (linking the previous quotation to the topic sentence above)
5) repeat #2-4 for 1 or 2 more quotations
6) concluding sentence

V.   Introduction

1) 1-2 general sentences about the text(s) or issue(s) you will discuss
2) 2-3 sentences about your general topic (i.e. heroic characters, the effects of the setting, etc.)

3) 1 sentence narrowing your discussion toward your thesis

4) conclude with your thesis statement (yes – 1 sentence!)

5) the introduction is an upside-down shape (from general to specific)

VI.   Conclusion

1) 1-2 sentences restating your main points / thesis

2) 2-4 sentences explaining how your thesis relates to the larger issues in the text(s)

    (i.e. Imagine a paper discussing the weapons used by the heroes in <u>Harry Potter and the Sorcerer's Stone</u> and <u>The Fellowship of the Ring</u> and how those weapons strengthen the heroism of Harry and Frodo. In the conclusion, you may reflect on some modern novels' / films' use of heroic weapons and how this technique is used throughout the ages. Your grade on these papers will be based largely on the connections you make. The best papers make connections in the conclusion as well. Admittedly, this is the hardest part of the essay to produce).

VII.   Format

1) the entire essay is double-spaced (from your name in the heading to the last sentence of your conclusion)

2) on the top left-handed side of page 1, the 1st line will have your name, the 3rd line your class (ENG I), the 5th line your teacher (Mr. Pawlyk), and the 7th line the date

3) on the 9th line, you'll have a centered title (which is connected to your thesis - - absolutely avoid titles like "Harry Potter Paper" or "English Thesis Paper")

4) your introductory paragraph will be indented (hit "tab" once) and will start on the 11th line)

VIII.   Proofreading

1) Proofread the essay yourself out-loud (note: if you don't proofread aloud, don't waste your time doing it silently!) -- make sure you mark the errors as you read

2) be sure the essay has gone through "spell-check"

3) no contractions (i.e. "can't, don't," etc.)

4) no slang (i.e. "socialize" rather than "hang out" / "fashionable" rather than "cool")

5) no baby verbs (i.e. variations of "to go, to make, to do," etc.)

6) minimal linking verbs (i.e. no more than 1 or 2 per paragraph)

7) no use of the word "thing" (a complete waste of ink!)

8) no 1st person used in the essay ("I, we," etc.)

9) no fragments (incomplete sentences - - proofreading aloud will help here)

10) correct usage of its, it's / to, two, to / there, their, they're

11) correct usage of the semicolon (make sure that the clauses on BOTH sides of the semi-colon can also be sentences)

12) <u>HAVE ANOTHER PERSON PROOFREAD IT</u> (preferably a better writer than you)

IX.   DUH!

13) Print it out and read it again (I'm serious!)

14) Staple it – *include checklist*

15) Put it in a place where it will not be forgotten

needs some work

good job

Artifact #26

The Boy Code

A ninth-grade class at an all-male private high school has been reading William S. Pollack's *Real Boys*.[1] The class spends one class session on Pollack's description of the *boy code*—an implicit set of rules and standards that guide the general behavior of many boys in our society. In the first part of the lesson, the teacher describes four aspects of the boy code and the students take notes. Later, the teacher and students work together to create a "web" of interrelated ideas about the boy code. One student's notes from the class appear on the next two pages.

Questions to Consider as You Examine the Notes

- Look at the first page of notes the student has taken during the teacher's lecture. How complete do these notes appear to be? Can you get a good sense of Pollack's concept of *boy code* simply by reading these notes? What strategies does the student use to enhance the usefulness of his notes?

- Now look at the web of ideas that the class has created. In what ways does the web supplement the student's original notes?

- The teacher has had the class construct the web as a group. In what ways might this strategy be more effective than asking students to construct their own, individual webs?

- What might the teacher's objectives be for the lesson? Speculate on the lesson's effectiveness in helping students accomplish those objectives.

---

[1] *Real Boys: Rescuing Our Sons From the Myths of Boyhood*, by W. S. Pollack, 1999, New York: Henry Holt.

Relate to → The Boy Code

Pollak said... 1) Every boy knows about it

2) Every man remembers it

3) Every woman can recognize it in men they know

2nd [If boys don't live up to the boy code they are...]

1) are shamed

2) are ashamed

3) establish a mask

4 STEPS OF BOY CODE

1) ~~Sturdy Oak~~

1) Sturdy Oak

acting job ⎱   - Do not grieve openly   ⎱ Signs of male
drains ⎰   - Don't show weakness   ⎰ instability and
energy   - Don't ask questions when confused ⎰ dependence

2) Give em Hell

- Guys are hard wired to be macho, violent, high energy (fights)

3) The Big Wheel

- Belief guys feel compelled to achieve status (need bigger cooler toys

- Forces boys to put on "Mask of Masculinity"

4) No Sissie Stuff

- Boys can't express any feelings seen as femine

- scared, empathy, warmth

- leads to premature seperation from parents

[WHERE DO WE LEARN THE BOY CODE?]

- ADULTS, MEDIA, CHILDREN

[3. MYTHS OF BOYHOOD]

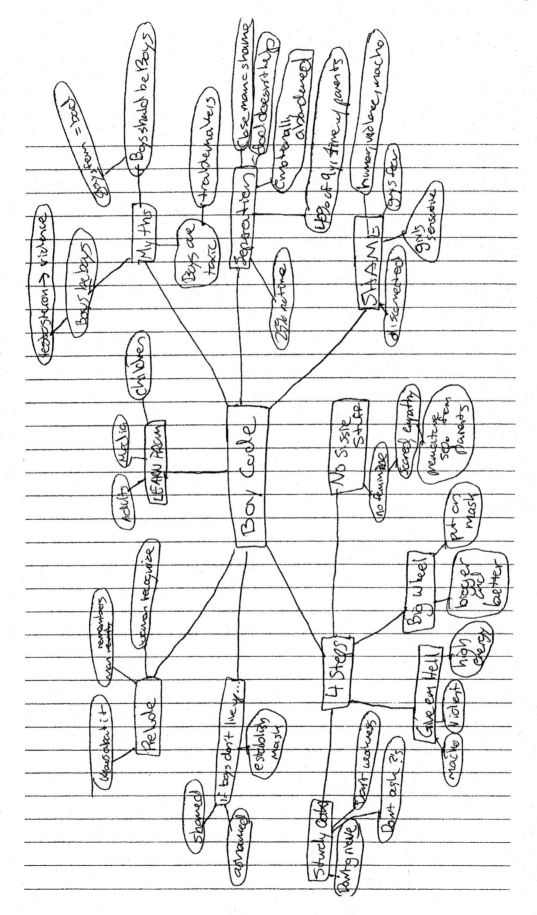

Artifact #27

Shadowing

At 14-year-old Connor's high school, one of the graduation requirements is to follow, or *shadow*, three different adults during a typical work day. For one such shadowing activity, Connor tags along when a prominent sports writer visits summer training camp for Denver's professional football team, the Broncos.

That evening, Connor writes a three-page reflection on his experience, which appears on the next three pages. He e-mails a copy to the journalist, who responds enthusiastically to what Connor has written and commends him on his creativity, sense of humor, and ability to tell a complete story.

Questions to Consider as You Examine the Composition

- What benefits might such a shadowing assignment have? Justify your answer by drawing on one or more theories of learning and motivation.

- Which aspects of Connor's shadowing experience are probably most valuable? Justify your choices.

- Connor intentionally chooses an informal, "playful" font for his word processing document. Is this appropriate for a school assignment? Why or why not?

My Day as a Journalist

It was no ordinary day. It started out like any other except for the feeling in my stomach—stress. It was a good kind of stress, though. I was excited to get up. Most Saturdays I sleep late and move slowly. This one saw me up at 6 AM because I could not wait. I was going to shadow a sports writer.

A few weeks earlier I met Richard ____ at a family picnic in California. Richard and I talked about football for a long time. When he told me he covered the Broncos for USA Today and that he would be in Greeley I was very excited. USA Today is the only paper started for the sole purpose of being a national newspaper. Richard covers the western NFL, which includes the Seahawks, the Cardinals, the 49ers the Raiders, Chargers, and my favorite-- the Broncos. It was sweet when Richard e-mailed my Dad to invite me to accompany him on his job for a day.

My dad and I met Richard at the media center. Richard and I started out in the pressroom where the pops and pastries are free and you have every book you would need to know about the

Broncos. There I got the key to the kingdom—my press pass. With that I could almost go anywhere in Bronco training camp.

Then we went to look at the Bronco's practice. The Broncos were doing drills. It was kind of repetitive and hot. We could not have our cell phones on during the whole practice. Richard introduced me to many journalists, including Sam Adams from the paper in Boulder. I asked most of the journalists who they thought would win the Super Bowl. Most said Ravens or Broncos Vs. Rams or Buccaneers. Richard also introduced me to the whole Bronco press and security staff.

After practice, all the players ran into the locker room. I met the Offensive Coordinator, Gary Kubiak, on his way to the locker room. Richard asked him about the three running backs and which of them would start. Gary said they all looked good and it felt like a college—there was a deep pool of talent. Then we talked to Desovin Fonte. Richard asked him if we could talk to him later. Then I saw Mike Shanahan, arguably the greatest mind in football. I did not know that Richard and Mike were good friends. Richard asked him about Terrell Davis and what happened to his latest injury. After that, we went to the pressroom where we talked to fellow reporters about Davis and his latest injury.

After the practice, all the players were leaving for the day. Then Mr. Fonte and Richard talked about his career. He has played for many leagues including the unsuccessful XFL and the CFL; now he is in the NFL on the Broncos and has a chance to start for the Denver Broncos. This is cool because he holds the record for most years in then out of the NFL.

Many of the reporters and players gave me advice. The funniest and most helpful was to keep your ears open and your mouth shut. As a reporter, your job is to learn from others—not to give your own point of view. The chance to express yourself comes later, in writing.

After we departed, Richard rode his bike back to his hotel and took a nap. That evening, he had to write his report for the newspaper. There was no time to mess around. Reporters like Richard learn to put themselves in a zone where they can write and meet deadlines. That is something I have not yet learned. But I did learn a lot. And I want to learn more.

Artifact #28

The War of 1812

Ms. Jensen's eleventh-grade U.S. history class is studying the War of 1812. The students each have responsibility for learning about a particular situation or event related to the war or to circumstances leading up to it. Then, in 10- to 15-minute oral presentations, students teach their classmates what they have learned.

Seventeen-year-old twins Jonathan and Adam give their presentations on the same day. Jonathan talks about the Warhawks, a group of men with considerable influence in Congress in the early 1800s. Adam describes the Battle of Tippecanoe and its impact on the war's outcome. Both boys distribute handouts listing key points they want their classmates to learn about their respective topics. These handouts are presented on the next two pages.

Questions to Consider as You Examine the Handouts

- What kinds of things have the boys focused on as they have read and learned about the Warhawks and the Battle of Tippecanoe?

- Based on what you see in the handouts, what might you infer about the boys' learning strategies? What might you infer about their *epistemological beliefs* about history—in other words, their beliefs about what it means to learn and "know" history?

- Are the learning strategies and epistemological beliefs you've identified typical of high school students? Defend your answer.

- What are the advantages of preparing such handouts for a class presentation? In particular, what advantages might the handouts have for (a) the student giving the presentation, (b) other students in the class, (c) the teacher? Are there any downsides to such handouts?

- Both boys use bulleted lists to present what they have learned. What alternative organizational structures might students use?

- How might a teacher help students create effective handouts?

The
WARHAWKS

- A group of men that dominated congress at the time of the war of 1812.

- Henry Clay from Kentucky and John C. Calhoun from South Carolina were the leaders of the Warhawks.

- Henry Clay was the speaker of the House of Representatives at the time before and during the War of 1812.

- The other Warhawks were Felix Grundy and John Porter.

- The Warhawks are a group of men who went all around the country convincing people that the U.S. should go to war.

- The Warhawks also spoke of conquering other people and expanding the country.

- People of New England opposed war because they thought a war with Britain would ruin there trade which had already been damaged.

- Also New Englanders sympathized with Britain and there struggle with Napoleon which is why some of them opposed the war.

- Some people believe that the Warhawks purpose was mainly to expand and take more land away from the indians.

- This was settled at the battle of Tippecanoe.

- The Warhawks reason for encouraging war was they heard that British officers from Canada were encouraging the Indians to rebel against the United States.

- One of the goals of the Warhawks was to take Canada.

- They also wanted Florida from the Spanish.

The Battle of Tippecanoe

- US troops vs. Shawnee Indians
- November 7, 1811
- Near Wabash and Tippecanoe Rivers
- Tecumseh leader of Shawnees
- "Prophet" Tecumseh's brother
- Forming intertribal confederacy against US occupation of lands ceded by the Indians in the Treaty of Fort Wayne signed in 1809
- William Henry Harrison was the governor of the Indian Territory
- Harrison took 950 soldiers and attacked the Shawnee encampment near Prophets town
- Tecumseh was not present during the attack
- The next morning the Shawnees' attacked and annihilated the US troops but after hours of fighting the US drove the natives out of the field
- Harrison lost 185 men
- Shawnee lost many more
- Harrison burnt Prophet town
- Called the "Great Victory"
- Helped Harrison become president in 1840

Dropping Out

For a district-wide writing assessment, the public schools of the Commonwealth of the Northern Mariana Islands (located north of Guam in the Pacific Ocean) asks eleventh graders to write an essay about the causes and potential effects of dropping out of school before graduating from high school. One student writes the essay presented on the following two pages.

The school district has developed standards that it uses to evaluate students' essays, including the following:

> [Students] use standard conventions of English appropriate to the selected audience.

> [Students] use knowledge and experience to write in an engaging, clear, and focused manner. Components include: thesis statement, main idea and supporting details; appropriate voice, interesting contexts; closure and resolution.[1]

Applying such standards, raters give each scorable essay a score ranging from 1 (Basic) to 4 (Advanced). A scoring manual provides a detailed set of criteria and examples of essays at each writing level that guide the raters in their judgments.

Questions to Consider as You Examine the Essay

- How well has the student planned and organized her thoughts? How clearly does she communicate her ideas and arguments? Does the student have adequate writing skills for a high school graduate?

- To write well, a student must also *think* well. What can you infer about the student's thinking skills by reading her essay?

- How convincing is the student's case for staying in school until high school graduation? From her perspective, what are the benefits of a high school education? If you were a high school student who was deciding whether to drop out, would the student's arguments convince *you* that it was important to stay in school? Why or why not?

- Drawing from the student's discussion of the reasons why students drop out, identify at least three different strategies that educators might use to help potential drop-outs stay in school.

---

[1] Excerpted from *Commonwealth of the Northern Mariana Islands–Public School System WRITING ASSESSMENT GRADE 11 Scoring Manual* (p. 2) by R. H. Inos, 2002, Commonwealth of the Northern Mariana Islands: Public School Systems. Reprinted by permission.

In life you have to take certain steps in order to be successful in life. For example School prepares you for the future. For example If you go to school, the school teaches you how to write in formal essays, teaches you how to do math, and teaches you other helpful things in life that you may need to be successful.

One cause of not finishing High school is dropping out or withdrawal from school. Here are some reasons' why I think students drop out. Some students may think It is cool to drop out from school, but they don't know what they are missing and what they could have been if they stayed in school. Some students may drop out because they have to work. For example they might need to work to support their child or maybe their parents need help with paying the bills or something.

Another cause of not finishing High school is taking foot steps of family members or friends who did not finish High school. Some students may think that just because their parents did not finish Highschool that it is okay to follow them in their foot steps, but these kinds of students don't think twice before they make their choice. For example, if a student stop schooling, he or she doesn't know what they could have be in the future.

The effects of not finishing High school is simple. If a person doesn't finish High school he or she may not beable to get a job, if he or she is able to get a job then they are lucky but their salary price would be low it wouldn'tl be low like that if they stayed in school and take their High school diploma.

In Conclusion to this essay I think it is better to stay in school and be somebody rather than dropout and be nobody. And I also think that principals' and teachers' should make school more fun and more interesting so that students could be more excited to come to school and more interesting to learn more.

Artifact #30

Common Standards

Oyster River High School in Durham, New Hampshire, has a list of "Common Standards" that guide learning and instruction across the curriculum. The standards are the result of a year-long effort in which, at a number of intensive work sessions, faculty, school administrators, students, parents, and community members brainstormed numerous ideas, pared them down into a workable number, tinkered with the wording to everyone's satisfaction, and grouped them into seven general categories.

The standards, which the school posted throughout the school building and distributed to all faculty, students, and parents, are presented on the following page.

Questions to Consider as You Examine the Standards

- To what extent do the standards focus on lower-level versus higher-level skills?

- If your textbook offers guidelines for developing instructional goals and objectives, are these standards consistent with those guidelines?

- Which standards lie within the cognitive domain? the psychomotor domain? the affective domain?

- What effects are the standards apt to have on teachers' instructional practices? What effects are they apt to have on students' learning and studying strategies?

- To what degree, and in what ways, are the standards likely to influence assessment practices in individual classrooms and for the school as a whole?

COMMON STANDARDS

The Oyster River High School learning community has high academic and performance standards. The common standards are a statement of the expectations which are supported across the curriculum. We are committed to working toward these standards as partners in learning.

- Learning strategies
  - Define task to be accomplished
  - Locate and extract relevant information from a wide variety of sources
  - Listen effectively
  - Read with comprehension
  - Follow directions and use time effectively
  - Demonstrate knowledge and skills in a variety of assessments

- Thinking
  - Analyze, evaluate and synthesize information
  - Distinguish between fact and opinion
  - Consider the causes and the short- and long-term effects of decisions and actions
  - Understand the influences of media and other forms of communication on our thoughts and actions
  - Appreciate the historical, current, and future contexts of issues and events
  - Create connections across diverse domains
  - Relate to a variety of creative forms of expression

- Problem solving
  - Identify problems and develop solutions and alternatives
  - Apply knowledge and skills appropriately
  - Use quantitative tools effectively
  - Utilize a systems approach in decision-making

- Communication
  - Speak with clarity and confidence
  - Ask appropriate questions, listen, and participate productively in discussions
  - Present information and ideas in a thorough and engaging manner
  - Utilize appropriate spelling and grammar in context
  - Produce clear, detailed, and well-organized writing
  - Use a variety of creative forms of expressions

- Wellness
  - Recognize the value of a healthy mind in a healthy body
  - Identify and use strategies for maintaining personal, community and environmental health

- Technology
  - Select appropriate technology for a task
  - Utilize technology to arrange, consider and present data
  - Understand both the potential and the limitations of technology

- Citizenship
  - Demonstrate respect and courtesy in personal interactions
  - Act responsibly and honestly
  - Set and plan for achievement of personal goals
  - Work cooperatively and constructively in groups
  - Respect diversity
  - Develop advocacy skills in interpersonal and public settings
  - Recognize interrelatedness in and responsibilities for the local and world community

These standards may be modified as appropriate for students with disabilities. For example, a disabled student's failure to satisfy these standards does not necessarily signify that the child's program is inappropriate if the child is nevertheless making educational progress.

Adopted 5/12/99